To Ko
Thank you for your support
you Enjoy

# Love &
# Other Monsters

Blue Fae Press
a division of Urban Book Editor LLC
PO Box 390665
Snellville, GA 30039

Love & Other Monsters

Copyright © 2016 by Kay B., Nina Brav, and Michelle Bishop
c/o Urban Book Editor LLC

ISBN (10): 0-9861519-1-2
ISBN (13): 978-0-9861519-1-0

Manufactured in the United States of America.

Illustrations by: Dwayne Johnson of Designs by DJ

Book Layout & Design: Urban Book Editor LLC
Editing: Urban Book Editor LLC

For more info and paperback copies email: info@urbanbookeditor.com
or visit http://www.urbanbookeditor.com/

# Dedication

This book is dedicated
to the monsters who inspired us,
the love that sometimes broke us, and
the one little man who never lets us down.

# Table of Contents

# Acknowledgments

We would like to thank all of the ancestors, for we are only here because we stand on their shoulders. We wish to thank the Most High for giving us the hearts and minds to feel, think, and write. We wish to thank our wonderful graphic designer, Dwayne Johnson of Designs by DJ, not only for developing artwork that encapsulated the essence of what we were trying to convey, but for doing so with grace and equanimity even when we had to be driving him absolutely nuts.

We would like to thank our teams of early readers who let us text them poems and passages at all hours of the day and night, especially E. Kelly and B. Everett, who survived many iterations of this project. Thank you to a very special Auntie M, who always seems a little shocked when we do something cool like this, but supports us anyway.

Thank you to the friends throughout the years who have offered support and guidance, with a special shout out to Anna P, who taught us that the human body is clearly made of peanut butter, which makes Uncrustables a required food group for our survival. Thank you to the men and women in our lives, both past and present, who have been helping us learn what we do (and do not) want or need from love.

On a personal note, I would like to thank my beautiful, amazing, strong, and incredibly intelligent children who have tolerated all levels of chaos and mayhem as we completed this project. It's us against the world, always and forever, Baby Boo Boos. Thank you for having my back. I've got yours until the bitter end.

On behalf of all of us, I send you love and blessings.

Michelle Bishop
*March 2016*

# Foreword

*"To love and to be loved is the first desire of every soul. To be understood is the second."* m.b.

Everyone wants love. It is the core of all human interaction. The young man who hires the mariachi to serenade his intended seeks love as does the woman who opens her heart and body to her lover.

Yet, beyond the desire for love is the desire for understanding. This is even more elusive and, in some ways, runs contrary to what we are taught about love. True love is meant to be unconditional, according to popular thought. Unconditional implies one need not be understood to be loved, that the highest expression of love is to love with complete faith and acceptance without the need to understand the object of one's love. Yet, the human spirit seems to seek that understanding. It is ironic. The two things we most crave seem to negate one another.

Perhaps the truth is more complex. Do we desire to be both loved and understood? Maybe we are seeking to be loved *in spite of* that understanding.

Love & Other Monsters explores the search for love from the perspectives of three women at different stages of life – a girl discovering romantic love for the first time, a young woman new to adulthood experiencing the volatility that comes with passionate relationships and heartbreak, and a middle-aged woman who has won and lost in love more than once and seeks to rediscover her joy. Through these women's voices, we see love blossom and evolve through physical desire to soaring adoration, to heart-rending pain and, eventually, to peace and acceptance. The heart wants what the heart wants, but the brain learns the heart doesn't always get its desires.

Still, the poems in Love & Other Monsters are not morose or depressing. They are at intervals hopeful, contemplative, and playful. Love & Other Monsters is an examination of love, desire, and loss. Each poem carries us through personal explorations of love tying together universal themes, finally bringing us back to ourselves with love and understanding.

Enjoy.

Michele A. Barard, *Editor*
Urban Book Editor LLC

On The Playground

## Wishes to the Sky

Far above, in a sea of black
With tiny glimmers that light
The night's path
Playful stars laugh
Mocking the nameless, faceless
Ones below who attach
Wishes to the sky

Different in size and body
A small silent whisper
A loud raging plea
Sweet like a toffee to your tongue
Rough as sandpaper to your skin
The selfish, the selfless
All unique
All alike

This chorus of ferocious laughter,
As stars zip across the sky,
Brightens the night
It lights paths for lost sailors,
And moonlit lovers, gives comfort to
Late night wonderers,
And all the dreamers
Hands curled, eyes shut, carelessly tossing
Their wishes to the sky

Behind closed eyes
Dreamers may wish but
With closed eyes they cannot see
Better are the
Doers, eyes open, present,
Taking play dough wishes
Pealing them from the sky
Shaping them into action

Nina Brav

## Not Kid Stuff

Take a breath.

Sometimes in life not everything is so easy
Like picking daisies from Nana's garden
and crowning ourselves queens, easy.
Baking chocolate chunk cookies
for the community center bake sale
and licking the bowl clean, easy.
But that was all kid stuff.
*This is serious.*

We have to help her.

I had a dream about her last night.
She was trapped, not like in a box
or a closet but across a vast ocean.
She can't swim. She wasn't here in pre-k when we all learned.
Trapped. We dug all day using anything we could find –
flat rocks, branches. We even took spoons from the cafeteria.
All day and all week we dug, hoping to reach her-
To be able to grab our friend and say,
"It's going to be alright. You're safe."

Then today, we came out
Went to our station beneath the jungle gym...
I actually cried real tears when I saw
Our hole. Our hole was filled.
Someone had filled our hole.
Someone had ruined our one chance.
My hands cradled my face. What to do?
I was devastated. What to do?
"What do we do?" a voice asked.
I stared blankly into my palms.
"Gabby, what do we do?"

*Not everything in life is so easy,* I told myself.
*It isn't kid stuff. This is real life--a mission.*
"We dig," I said. And we did.
And if someone filled it up, we dug again, faster.
This mission, this goal was not easy and it wasn't kid stuff.
That didn't matter.
By the end of it I knew in my heart that we would do it.
I knew in the end we would have our hole to China.

Nina Brav

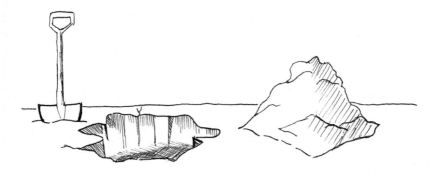

## In Childhood's Hour

Copied lines
into a spiraled,
yellow notebook
Never realizing
they foreshadowed
loneliness, other-ness,
outside-ness, blankness...
What is it to know so young
you are not as others are?
As a very child to feel
the weight and gloom
of a world unclear,
full of dreadful
demons walking
in the sunlight?

m.b.

## The Tightrope Walker

Walking a tightrope between two worlds,
A girl of both constantly told to choose
Simply trying to keep herself from falling
"You're so lucky to fit in everywhere," they'd say
Not knowing that fitting in meant never truly being
Tired of living in a black and white world
When she, herself, is a shade of grey
Each day a struggle to keep from plummeting to Earth
Juggling the expectations of herself and those around her
From a young age knowing there is no net
Stuck balancing above the world as the Circus of Life keeps moving
Full of masks and acts that hide the truth
Of all the pain we pretend not to feel.
All around her many shows go on:
Clowns with painted faces and forced smiles,
Contortionists twisting and bending to make others happy,
Acrobats terrified to show just how close they are to slipping.
Each takes place under a different tent
All too focused on their own performances
To see beyond the crowd
She pretends not to feel the stares of the audience
Not knowing her greatest fear is falling before them
At the end of the night the crowd retreats
The lights shut off
Only she remains
Still trying to keep her balance

Kay B.

- 17 -

## Philodendron

Queen Marble Fern
Is how I learned your name
Tough little creature that you are...
No matter how I tried
No water
No light
No attention
Moving from place to place
Certainly no tender speech
*Nothing* managed to kill you
Until one day
When I realized how much I loved
To have you there
Not demanding anything from me at all
I looked again only to find
You slumped over
In desperate need
Of great feeling and deep words

m.b.

## I Wish...

*"I wish to close my eyes and see only my dreams." – Kay B.*

I wish
to be free to live as I choose, to live among the stars,
to dance with faeries in the wind

I wish
Each day was not a psychic battle
One side believing that hope is naught, the other begging to
never give up

I wish
there were no nights in which the darkness rose
striking deafening blow after deafening blow upon an already
battered heart

I wish
I were cold and calloused so none could capture my heart
And watch a fool be made in pitiful attempts to gain favor

I wish I were not so scared
I wish I would not forget the joy
I wish I did not need wishes

Kay B.

## Moonlight

I bathe you in my light and watch you wander
warily checking over your shoulders
Fearful
of night animals scurrying, calling
to one another through the woods
Dreading
leaving your comforts –
electric lights, televisions, computers
Those new night sounds,
so different from the ancient calls of
owls and crickets and all manner of wild thing
roaming the forests you used to know
Long ago
my light marked the passing of time,
lit the way as you moved confidently through the night
A time long past you honored me –
creator of all, symbol of life – and death
Now distant,
removed from me and from yourselves,
the time before merely a memory
But once in a while,
when feeling romantic or filled with nostalgia,
you are drawn into the night
For a short while you bask in my light
and I shine upon you – with love

m.b.

## Night Waltz

Stars grace the peaceful night
Attending the ball in the sky
Where they dance and sway,
Trying to outdo each other
All to gain the attention of the moon,
Who enchants them with her silent beauty.

The rare star takes a chance and dives across the sky,
Leaving behind a streak of light, dazzling all who dare look.
He is encouraged by wishes and desires of dreamers below.
Still, despite the best effort of even the most charming of stars,
The moon spares not a glance, only ever staring at the horizon.
The moon's heart was captured long ago.

Each day she awaits a glimpse of her beloved
Once upon waking and again before drifting to sleep.
Only twice a year do their paths cross
When they finally meet and share a kiss each second cherished
She eagerly awaits the next time they may be in each other's arms.

Kay B.

## Holding on to Daisies in the Moonlight

Moonlight peaked from navy skies
Stars lit an endless path.
Two youths, too young, gazed stars above
And wished their love could last.

'Twas summer time, the air was warm
They lied beneath the giant oak
She plucked a daisy from the ground
They smiled and laughed and joked

The two so fresh, rose in their eyes
They could not see the clouds
To be together always was
The only thing allowed

One month from now that boy she loved
Was leaving for the war
She'd stay behind all by herself
To dream of times before

Fire and steal can tear through skin
And blood can flow through sand
Against the Oak that stands so tall
Could lean her dying man

But that night the sky was far too bright
And weather far too warm
To think of sadness yet to come
And someone yet to mourn

They smiled and kissed and shared their love
As only youths know how
And though one day he would be gone
That night they'd think of now.

Nina Brav

## On the Playground

Jumping on my bike
Clear skies, golden light overhead
Wind whipping up
Freedom in my soul
Speeding toward green patches
With swings and slides
*How I loved the swings*
That ability to simply by
Pumping back and forth
Go higher and higher
Soaring toward the clouds
Not always safe to go out alone
Walking to the 7-11 for a soft drink and candy
Or to the bus stop to go to
Grandma's house or the shopping mall
Drinks thrown on freshly pressed uniforms
Elderly white men offering wrinkled candy
Better to ride to the playground
Pump thick brown thighs
Back and forth, eyes closed,
Kissed by the sun

m.b.

## Mother's Warning

"Stay close – close to the trees that stand firm in the ground and grip the night sky. With the tip of their branch, twigs outstretched like fingers, they grasp for even the tiniest thread from the endless cloak above. Stay close, Dear. Do not wander. Do not stray."

Nina Brav

## Silly or Young

How silly I was then
Or maybe too young
To see the darkness on the wall
Was just myself
Reflected.

The wooden night light
That carved the image of a withered tree
Standing still in moonlight
That's what made it bigger

That's why I was afraid.

So I cowered under covers,
Silly to think a blanket
Could shield me from my monster
Too young to know
I'd never really
escape it.

Nina Brav

Keep Digging

Love and Other Monsters

## Date Night

She fumbled with her keys as they got to the door.
"I had a really not terrible night tonight."
"I had a not terrible night too."
He smiled.
She paused. Her heart beat at such a normal rate she hardly
noticed it in her chest.
"Well," she opened the door slowly, "good night."
"Let me grab that for you."
His hand glazed over hers and for a slight second they stood still,
eyes locked.
She turned her head, brushing a single escaped curl back behind
her ear.
"Thank you."
As the door closed behind her she blew a kiss.
*Not a terrible night at all*, she thought as she walked down the
hallway towards her apartment.

Nina Brav

## Envy the Stars

Each night I envy the stars for they may
Gaze upon her beauty while I may only dream
Of eyes ever full of warmth and compassion
That show the kindness of her soul
Her beauty is such that I forget how to speak
And only watch in awe as she grants me a smile.

Surely she knows not of my feelings
But, oh, how I wish she did!
She is neither my lady nor my love
Yet my pulse quickens in her presence
And if I shall compare her to a summer's day
The summer shall wither in defeat
Before I even begin to speak.

I love to bait her with words and watch
Her eyes alight in mirth though
She assumes a guise of outrage.
Each moment with her is like
Losing all feeble ties to gravity
And dancing among the gods.

I had long ago given up wishing yet
She inspires me and fills me with hope
Thus I find myself wishing each day
That she might take that ever terrifying step
And fall into my waiting arms.

Kay B.

## Nothing

Swooning youth
What will you be
In the morning?

After passion eats
Away at your soul
And the restless night whispers
Sweet toothless nothings.

Perhaps you'll learn
Of the unspoken treasure buried
Deep below
Layers of smooth tissue and doubt.

If lucky (though few are)
You'll get back the gift of sight,
The one you enjoyed thoughtlessly,
While skipping rope and climbing trees.

Most likely you'll get nothing,
The same nothing you would have
Without the loathing black seductress of the sky,
The moon, without the lustful stars.

The same nothing
As when you wake up,
Cool and damp,
From a dream you almost, but can't, remember.

Incomplete but not missing
There's nothing to miss
When you can't remember.

Nina Brav

## Spartacus

Thine kiss upon my lips
Would leave me lustful,
Would make hands wander,
Though not sure if before or after thoughts.

Just a kiss would
Make me crumble to the dirt
Weakened, unhindered by inhibitions
Inflamed by thirst that could be
Quenched only by thine divinity.

My mouth upon thine own
Would set the world aflame.

To yearn for one so deeply –
A retched fate.
But better to burn in embrace than to
Watch lonely soul wither in darkened nights.

Nina Brav

## There's Something about December

Something about her catches his eye.
Maybe it's the playful ways she pulls at the string of her
sweatshirt. Or maybe it's how she blows kisses to strangers or
keeps her hair in front of her face.
Perhaps it is her eyes – icy blue like his favorite freezer pop that
comes in the plastic. She was cold. She was cruel. She was his
perfection and the stick thin object of my disdain.

Nina Brav

## Maybe Today

Maybe today
he will bring me flowers, hold me close,
kiss me until I've no breath
Maybe today
he will take my hand, call me sweetheart,
declare unending love –
Certainly tomorrow

m.b.

## Midnight

Blood stained river leads
my way. "Follow the water,"
he would always say.

As gentle wind hugs
sun kissed skin, for a moment
I forgot the war.

Nina Brav

## Truth

Slippery as an eel
Elusive as the elves
That steal only one sock
From each load of laundry
Is there clarity, understanding, or
Light as I look into your face?
Watching the words form,
Listening for, but never actually hearing,
The truth

m.b.

## Lucky Penny

She threw the rice at him.
Tiny grains floating through air
Well-meaning by nature but
Now her weapon of attack.

"Liar!" she yelled.
Little plums
Blossomed on her cheeks,
Her eyes sewn shut
With adhesive rage—
The single barricade between her and the rain.

"Lying scum." She threw a tin at him.
It bounced playfully off his slick,
Parted hair.
His eyes were a shallow well,
Meaningful only to the clumsy girl
Who had trusted him with a lucky penny.

"Liar," she puffed out with a quiet exhale.
She sat, silently
Unbuckled her shoes,
And removed them.

Then she got up and walked.

And as she walked down those stairs,
Away from the broken
Stained glass, the unlit
Candles, the unprayed prayers,
She stepped on the small grains.

Well meaning, but painful to her
Naked toes,
A weapon of her own design.

Nina Brav

## Without Warning

*Implosion of the soul generally occurs without warning. – m.b.*

So sudden
I could not anticipate
The extraordinary pain
From the gaping hole
In the center of my chest
Where my heart sat,
I had thought, safely nestled
Inside my rib cage
Cradled gently in soft tissue
And muscle until the day
I understood
That you never loved me and
Never would and
All those years
Of trying to be good
Didn't soften your heart
Instead, bred disdain
So you could easily rip
Mine to shreds over and over
'Til finally
Light dawned –
Not like soft candlelight –
More like sticks of dynamite
Strategically placed
Causing my soul to collapse upon itself

m.b.

## Around and Around

Round and round
We went on
Discussing
Debating
Deciding
The issue
Worn out
From the
Argument
That seemed
Never to end
As we
Decided
Debated
Discussed
And went on
Round and round

m.b.

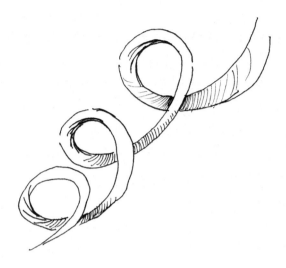

## Children Shouldn't Play with Dead Things

"It's dead," the little girl said as she pointed
'though I knew it already – had seen it before – in a dream
As I lay dying in my own sorrow
Bit by bit, pieces of my soul
Flaking off like old paint off the water-damaged
Front porch of the house by the lake
Where spirit led us
To expect sweet joy
Only to wallow in misery
Dead things arriving in nightmares and
In the front yard
Curled up like babies in their mothers' wombs

m.b.

## Dirty Hands

Soot on palms.
It adds an inch-thick layer to my blistered hands. Two hands
once tan, now worn, torn, and black from this evening's task.

The silver shines when it reflects the street light above. With
strength enough to keep a werewolf at bay and value enough
to adorn elites, tonight the metal serves only one purpose: to dig.

Bury, rather. A hole to fill with all of our unresolved fights,
unexplained anger, inconsistent episodes. That one time you
yelled and I shook with such anger and sadness that I dropped
the tea kettle. The other when we drove on Route 9, our ear
shattering silence booming with each bump in the road. When
you ripped my journal and I burned your favorite tie... All buried,
soon to be packed by this precious metal and covered with the
very soot that's caked onto the creases in my palm.

The world around me is still. The only two sounds are my
breath and the clank of the shovel at work. As the metal hits
earth, I wonder how long until I finally can wash off the dirt from
my tired hands.

Nina Brav

## As My Eyes Prepare to Rest

"It's late. I have to tend to my dreams," she said.
"Your dreams?" He took a long drag from his cigarette.
"Of course. If I don't, who will?" She chuckled at her own joke.
He stared into the vast black behind the
window pane. He didn't know who tended to
dreams. He had never dreamed before.
She snatched up his cigarette and smashed the
end into the lonely saucer on their living room
table. "It's late."

Nina Brav

## 15

You appeared in my dream last night--
A dusty memory that shocked me to my core.
You smiled your devilish grin and,
suddenly, I was 15.

Your slimy words slithered into me,
"Great to see you...," they hissed,
"Can I see you again before I leave?"
The black pit rolling around in my stomach got bigger.
"Sure," I managed
– In fell my lungs.

After I walked away,
Shocked from having seen you
for the first time in so long,
I cried. Well, dream me cried.

My dream self-mourned
for the broken-hearted youth you left behind
so many years ago
in your trail of destruction.

The poor young girl who, apparently,
still lives inside me – fifteen, weak, and broken
gripping her insecurities like an even younger me
might've gripped my stuffed dog's paw.

I woke up.
It was a dream. Of course, I woke up.
But the black pit never subsided
and my mind couldn't stop
lingering on the playful smile
and the gentle touch that burned
my cheek.
A scab, it seems, I picked raw
--aching, bleeding, fresh,
like when I was fifteen.

Nina Brav

## At Twilight

At twilight, work begins
Bulbous body, spindly legs
Spinning out the finest of threads
Intricately constructed
Ever-changing patterns that
Catch the light but
Never truly reveal the lady
Patiently awaiting her prey

m.b.

## Disenchantment

At first
It seemed
We were coming together
Naturally, rhythmically
Moving toward imperfect union

Dancing
Just the way
The stars and the planets
Slowly, gently
Undulate around the sun

Instead
We bump around
Clumsily, haphazardly
Not light on our feet
Without grace

m.b.

## And Then We Walked Away

We could have talked it over
worked through fears,
gaps in understanding,
but it seemed too much work to
pry at old walls
that made it possible for us
to remain aloof from the fact that
the house was falling down
around our ears.
We hadn't sense or
wherewithal to
save ourselves and all we'd built
so we stopped talking,
turned our backs,
and then we walked away.

m.b.

## Pensamientos de un Pescador

Attached by a small hook
Hangs the brightly colored painting
By the artist whose name is no longer recalled
That inspired such joy each day
Upon opening the eyes that it was carried
From home to home, city to city,
Even though the joy was no longer there
When gazed upon
The soul pondered the losses – so many losses
Attached to the times, the places, the people, the spaces
Where the bright colors once brought joy
Now, nothing

m.b.

## Still Broken

You think you're whole
When a whole half
– A whole half –
Of who you are belongs
To someone else.

What do you do when you still don't
want to take it back?

Who exactly do you belong to?

Nina Brav

## When He's Gone

I'll rejoice,
dance a jig,
drink a jug of wine,
and be grateful
for the headache
and dry mouth
I'll suffer the next day.
I'll sing a song,
make a prayer
of gratitude,
celebrate with friends,
make love to the nearest
able-bodied man,
or woman, if I'm drunk enough.
I'll go back to church –
finally forgiving God
for letting evil bastards
get away with being
evil bastards –
for never once punishing
for the multitude of indignities
imposed over the years.
Then, I'll sleep
the most peaceful sleep
one undisturbed
by pain, suffering, angst, or fear
for the first time
in many years

m.b.

## Working with the Left Hand

Wishes for good things
For children, husbands,
Mothers and selves
With the right hand
Drawing peace,
Prosperity, love, and jobs
All the things a person
Wants and needs
(So they think)
To be happy
Except when things go wrong
As they inevitably do
Then, they cry and cuss and spit
Begging for the work
Of the left hand
That hurts, binds, destroys,
And, yes, even kills
The joy, the home,
The family, the town
The destruction as large
And unexpected
As the hurricane sweeping over the land
Bringing water from the sky
And from the sea
To end all life
As they knew it

m.b.

## Lost Again

I'm feeling very lost right now.
I wonder, are you too?
It hit me rather suddenly
A fog wave passing through.

It floats at shoulder length, I think,
'Cause when I'm standing tall
And figuring which way to go
My instincts hit a wall.

But when I stick my head below,
As if to tie my shoe,
It's suddenly so clear to me
What I had planned to do.

The path I mapped out months ago
Is just some miles ahead
But stand back up and try to walk,
It just escapes
Again.

Nina Brav

## My Wicked Mistress

If ever I were to allow myself
To be beaten half-to-death again,
My will no longer my own,
Lost to that fateful enemy once more,
Do not pity me, simply scorn me for not
Stopping what I could have prevented.
For embracing what only time can cure,
If one has not already reached the point of madness.

I will have foolishly given in to my
Deepest wants and fallen to my mistress,
Truly forgetting that she is crueler
The more that I fight her. And when I give in
She walks me to the edge of the cliff
And kisses me goodbye as she silently
Begs me to jump and says she will be there to catch me;
That demon lies and allows me to plummet to my death.

She is too cruel to allow me to die in peace,
Thus she resurrects me and yet again spells me until
I have forgotten her wickedness and the pain it causes me
and I allow her to lead me to the cliff again.
I loathe her! She is my drug and I cannot
resist her. I am currently fighting her, but
Love is a strong and wily opponent,
Who constantly finds a way through my defenses.

Kay B.

Should I
Dance

Love and Other Monsters

## As the Sun Rises

In solitude but not alone
Between prayer, sleep, and vision
Learn ancient tongues
Secret lessons
Of herb, water, and spirit
The power of word
Oaths of silence
Strength renewed
Faith reinvigorated
Re-enter the world of mankind
As the Sun rises to
Meet the new you

m.b.

## Waiting

Hanging
Like the bed sheet
Out on the line
Longer than necessary to
Dry in the summer breeze
Flailing on the line
Day turning to twilight
Twilight to night
Waiting for dawn

m.b.

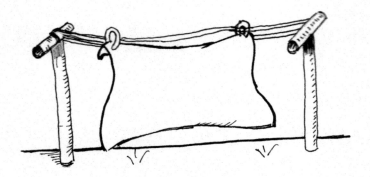

## Never Written

This is the love poem
I have never written
Because I always get stuck
Pondering the love

That came before
That didn't work out
When we broke each other's hearts
And bank accounts

When we lost our way
Lost the faith
Prayed for more
But got less

So much less but still hoped
Only to be disappointed again
In one another
In ourselves

m.b.

## If Only the Possibilities Were Not Endless

If only the possibilities were not endless
I would not be able to imagine
All the tiny and great things that
Pass through my mind each day we do not speak.
Was it the careless remark I made that day?
Or, the time I didn't answer the phone
When you called because
I was cleaning the bathroom and
Didn't hear the phone ring?
Or was it the ex-girlfriend
Who looked you up on Facebook and
Started reminiscing about old college days?
Or was it the ex-wife?
*It could have been the ex-wife.*
Or, could it be that I shared too much
Too soon and didn't make great efforts
To hide my flaws because it seemed
Disingenuous to pretend that I was perfect
When, well, who is?
Maybe you were abducted by aliens?
Wishful thinking, perhaps.
If you were abducted by aliens, then I could
Put to rest all the amazing, and not so amazing,
Ideas that scamper through my restless mind.

m.b.

## The Nights are the Hardest

*"The nights are the hardest," she'd said.*
*She was right.*

Night came. So did total destruction.
Dark winds howled, pushed me, dragged me off my perch, down
with a thud. Clay skin cracked, pieces of me spread across cold
cement floors. Then came the winged creatures. They tore at me,
scratching and ripping away until I was exposed. Night came after
me like a chisel, chipping into me until I was bloody, sore.

But in this pain, this sadness, this utter destruction, there's
something hopeful. My brokenness for the first time makes me
wonder, *What great work of art I am being re-chiseled into?*
*How much stronger might I be when I finally fill in the cracks in my*
*broken, dry skin?*

Nina Brav

## Martini Light

Not too dazed
To see through the shimmering light
You know – that special glow
Cast by cosmos and pineapple martinis

Not so confused
As to wander unprotected
Into unchartered lands with
Soldier boys – no longer quite boys

But off-center enough
To drunk dial – against all advice –
One most desired, too far away to touch
Memories still covered in stardust

m.b.

## Despacio

Instead of
Rushing away from
The love we'd lost
Like the rapid current of the
Yellow River
That curves behind the neighbor's house
Under the overpass and
Alongside the cemetery
We meandered
Out of each other's lives
More like
Bayou St. John
En route to the lake
Motion barely perceptible to the untrained eye
Which upon first glance
Would not likely notice the flow
Or imagine any movement at all
From bayou to lake
To canal to river
To gulf and finally
Out to sea

m.b.

## Shadow Man

I ache for an inkling of you –
a brief reminder
that I am not
alone.
Night light in my corner,
rays caressing shadows,
reminds me
gently
that I do not have to
fear
The Dark.

Nina Brav

## Laugh Lines

Face the same
Kind of, sort of,
Harder-edged than remembered
Formerly smooth
Now with deep creases
At the sides of the mouth
Except when he laughed,
Really laughed,
Then the boy, no – young man, I knew
Shined through
Glinting brown eyes
Tiny laugh crinkles at the corners
Harsh lines transformed
Almost their former selves
For just a moment of
Unrestrained joy

m.b.

## Positive Vibes

When right –
Love energy flows
Between us
Like the strongest
Electrical current
Carrying light
Into the heart
Of midnight

m.b.

## Black Leather and Red Carnations

It's easy to miss you when you're gone.
As I lay on crumbled sheets,
Lights dim, I look for your brown shoes
To be perfectly placed at the foot of my bed.
I want to run my finger tips
Along the black leather of your
Satchel, slightly worn and seated
Proudly on a chair.
I sniff, hoping the scent
Of your three cologne mix
Still lingers.
I close my eyes and imagine in just moments
I will hear that familiar
Tap, tap, tap
On my window.
No shoes to see, no bag to touch,
No scent to smell, or taps to hear.
Just the red carnations you left on my table.

Nina Brav

## Should I?

Should I...
take it personally, make excuses, or
weep over a bottle of red wine?

Because you...
were glad we connected again, enjoyed me, but
don't really care one way or another.

Or should I dance?

m.b.

## Just Beneath the Bed

Just beneath the bed
In a box tucked into the
Corner against the wall
Are all the memories –
Dancing, praying, eating, making love –
Making love was the hardest to shove into the box.
His touch had lingered for so long after he'd gone,
'though he'd sworn it'd be for just a short while.
He'd clearly lost his way or his sense of time
'Til after untold hours,
She left her perch by the window
Where she'd been waiting,
Found a small box, and placed each feeling inside.
*Carefully, now! You never know*
*When you're going to need them,*
She heard a small voice say.
She gathered them up
Packing each in one by one,
Taping the box tightly, and
Tossing it just beneath the bed.

m.b.

## Clouds the Mind

Nebulous, dark stormy thoughts
That in another space and time
Would have incited riotous rebellion
Now cloud the mind with fear, anxiety, self-doubt
Driving self-destructive pursuits
Wine, rum, sweets, and ... ah yes... sweets
Light finally breaking through
Confusion giving way to meditation, prayer, peace

m.b.

## Naked in the Rain

Sweet sun
Shining rays
Of happiness
Drip, like rain drops,
From umbrellas
That poorly cover
Naked souls.
Sunshine rain
Tickles skin --
Kissing,
Giving
A sense of
Hope, and
Love,
And
Belonging.

Nina Brav

## La Rosa con Espinas

Yellow with red edges
A single rose lifts herself out
Of the hard red clay,
Against dry conditions and lack of care.
Yet there she stands,
Stem arcing forward toward the light
Struggling against the wind
Looking, perhaps, as though
She does not deserve to stand
Yet stand she does, against the odds.

m.b.

Love and Other Monsters

# About the Authors

## Michelle Bishop

New Orleans native Michelle Bishop loves words, both written and spoken. Quite certain that she was a novelist, Michelle stumbled upon poetry and quickly discovered that it might, in fact, be her calling. Her experience living abroad in Mexico and Central America fuels her pursuit of cultural knowledge focusing on Afro-Caribbean and African Traditional Religions. These influences, as well as her experiences as a mother, an entrepreneur, and a divorcee, allow her to help others by sharing her hard-won wisdom in poetry and prose. Learn more about Michelle Bishop at www.MichelleBishopWrites.com.

## Nina Brav

Born and bred in the South, Nina Brav is a graduate of Boston University Questrom School of Business. She lives and works in Boston daylighting as a business consultant and moonlighting as a writer, blogger, and entrepreneur. Founder of A Nina Production, Nina explores a variety of writing styles, from fiction and poetry to vignettes and opinion essays. She views the world through a magical lens, which allows her to explore love, fear, and other monsters. One day, she believes, she might even conquer them. Learn more about Nina Brav at www.aninaproduction.com or @NinaBrav on Instagram and Facebook.

## Kay B.

Kay B, known better by those close to her as "Madam Waffle," was writing before she could even walk. A Romantic at heart, Madam Waffle's writing explores love and its effect on the human experience. Kay B lives, schools, and works in Atlanta, GA where she spends much of her time reading, writing, and designing lighting for theater productions. Learn more about Kay B at www.madamwaffle.com.

CPSIA information can be obtained
at www.ICGtesting.com
Printed in the USA
LVOW01s0004010416
481661LV00001B/1/P